OSCAR RUSSEL

EVERYDAY SPINACH RECIPES

THE COOKBOOK THAT WILL CHANGE THE MIND FOR THOSE WHO HATE VEGETABLES

Table of Contents

What are the 5 top health benefits of spinach?

May help maintain good vision

The dark green colour of spinach leaves indicates they contain high levels of chlorophyll and health-promoting carotenoids including beta carotene, lutein and zeaxanthin. As well as being anti-inflammatory and anti-cancerous, these phytonutrients are especially important for healthy eye sight, helping to prevent macular degeneration and cataracts.

May support energy levels

Spinach has long been regarded as a plant which can restore energy, increase vitality and improve the quality of the blood. There are good reasons for this, such as the fact that spinach is rich in iron. This mineral plays a central role in the function of red blood cells which help transport oxygen around the body, supports energy production and DNA synthesis. However, high levels of a compound called oxalic acid, naturally found in spinach, appears to inhibit the absorption of minerals like iron; that said, lightly cooking or wilting appears to minimise these effects.

May support heart health

Spinach, like beetroot, is naturally rich in compounds called nitrates; these may help improve blood flow and pressure by relaxing the blood vessels, reducing arterial stiffness and promoting dilation. A reduction in blood pressure helps reduce the risk of heart disease and stroke. Studies suggest that nitrate-rich foods, like spinach, may also help heart attack survival.

May support healthy bones

Spinach is an excellent source of <u>vitamin K</u> as well as being a source of <u>magnesium</u>, calcium and phosphorus. These nutrients are important for maintaining <u>bone health</u>.

May be protective

Spinach is loaded with protective compounds called polyphenols. Studies suggest, that along-with its vitamin content these compounds may promote cancer-protective properties. Animal studies suggest including spinach in the diet may protect against colon cancer.

Is spinach safe for everyone?

Spinach is safe for most people, however there are some individuals who need to exercise caution. Spinach contains a high amount of oxalate, for this reason people with a history of oxalate-containing kidney stones should minimise their consumption.

Those on blood-thinning medication need to consider their vitamin K intake. Typically, the advice, while taking this medication, is that you need to keep your dietary intake approximately the same. Check with your GP before making any significant changes to your diet.

Spinach Caramelized Onion And Muenster Au

Ingredients

8 red potatoes, cubed
5 ounces fresh spinach leaves
1/4 cup butter
1 onion, sliced
1 teaspoon minced garlic
3 tablespoons all-purpose flour
1/2 teaspoon salt
1 cup milk
1 cup heavy cream
2 cups shredded Muenster cheese

Directions

Preheat an oven to 400 degrees F (200 degrees C). Combine the potatoes and spinach in a 9x13-inch baking dish; set aside.

Melt 3 tablespoons of butter in a saucepan over medium-low heat. Stir in the onion, and cook until dark brown, about 15 minutes. Stir in the garlic and flour; cook 1 minute more. Season with salt, and stir in the milk and cream. Bring to a simmer over medium heat; cook and stir until the sauce has thickened, about 10 minutes. Stir in 3/4 of the Muenster cheese until melted, and pour over the potatoes.

Cover the potatoes with aluminum foil, and bake in the preheated oven 30 minutes. Uncover, and cook 20 minutes more, then sprinkle with the remaining Muenster cheese, return to the oven, and bake until the potatoes are tender and the cheese is bubbly, about 10 minutes more.

Warm Chicken Spinach Salad

Ingredients

3 cups torn fresh spinach
1 (11 ounce) can mandarin
oranges, drained
1/2 cup sliced fresh mushrooms
3 slices red onion, halved
1/2 pound skinless, boneless
chicken breast halves - cut into
strips
1/4 cup chopped walnuts
2 tablespoons olive or vegetable
oil
2 teaspoons cornstarch 1/2
teaspoon ground ginger 1/4
cup orange juice
1/4 cup red wine vinegar or cider
vinegar

Directions

On two salad plates, arrange spinach, oranges, mushrooms and onion; set aside. In a skillet, saute chicken and walnuts in oil until chicken is no longer pink. In a small bowl, combine the cornstarch, ginger, orange juice and vinegar until smooth; stir into the chicken mixture. Bring to a boil; cook and stir for 2 minutes or until thickened and bubbly. Pour over salads and serving immediately.

Spinach Dip With Cajun Pita Chips

Ingredients

cups sour cream
(10 ounce) package frozen
hopped spinach, thawed and
queezed dry
/4 cup finely chopped sweet red
epper
/4 cup chopped green onions
garlic clove, minced
/4 teaspoon salt
/4 teaspoon hot pepper sauce
CHIPS:
pita breads, halved and split
/2 cup butter, melted
/2 teaspoon Cajun seasoning
/4 teaspoon ground cumin

Directions

In a bowl, combine the sour cream, spinach, red pepper, onions, garlic, salt and hot pepper sauce. Cover and refrigerate for at least 1 hour.

Meanwhile, for chips, cut each pita half into four wedges. Combine the butter, Cajun seasoning and cumin; brush over rough side of pita wedges. Place on ungreased baking sheets. Bake at 400 degrees F for 8-10 minutes or until chips are golden brown and crisp. Serve with dip.

Spring Strawberry Spinach Salad

Ingredients

1 bunch spinach, rinsed
10 large strawberries, sliced
1/2 cup white sugar
1 teaspoon salt
1/3 cup white wine vinegar
1 cup vegetable oil
1 tablespoon poppy seeds

Directions

In a large bowl, mix the spinach and strawberries.

In a blender, place the sugar, salt, vinegar, and oil, and blend until smooth. Stir in the poppy seeds. Pour over the spinach and strawberries, and toss to coat.

Spinach, Artichoke and Crab Wontons

ngredients

cup mayonnaise
cup grated Parmesan cheese
cups shredded mozzarella
heese
(14 ounce) can artichoke hearts,
rained and chopped
/2 (10 ounce) package frozen
hopped spinach, thawed and
rained
/2 (6 ounce) can crabmeat
clove garlic, minced
/2 teaspoon onion powder
/4 teaspoon ground black
epper
/4 teaspoon ground white
epper
(16 ounce) package wonton
rappers
/2 cup diced green onion

Directions

Preheat an oven to 350 degrees F (175 degrees C). Mix mayonnaise, Parmesan cheese, mozzarella cheese, artichoke hearts, spinach, crabmeat, garlic, onion powder, black pepper, and white pepper in a bowl. Set aside.

Place wonton wrappers into mini muffin tins and bake in the preheated oven until lightly golden, about 5 minutes. Remove from oven and scoop about 1 teaspoon of the crab mixture into each wrapper. Return to the oven and continue baking until wontons are golden brown and the filling is hot, about 5 minutes more. Garnish with green onions and serve immediately.

Garlic, Spinach, and Chickpea Soup

Ingredients

2 tablespoons olive oil
4 cloves garlic, peeled and crushed
1 medium onion, coarsely chopped
2 teaspoons ground cumin
2 teaspoons ground coriander
1 1/3 quarts vegetable stock
3 medium potatoes, peeled and chopped
1 (15 ounce) can garbanzo beans, drained
1 cup heavy cream
2 tablespoons tahini
2 tablespoons corn meal
1/2 pound spinach, rinsed and chopped
ground cayenne pepper to taste
salt to taste

Directions

Heat olive oil in a large pot over medium heat, and stir in garlic and onion. Cook until tender. Season with cumin and coriander.

Mix vegetable stock and potatoes into the pot, and bring to a boil. Reduce heat, and simmer about 10 minutes. Stir in the garbanzo beans, and continue to cook until potatoes are tender.

In a small bowl, blend the heavy cream, tahini, and corn meal. Mix into the soup.

Stir spinach into the soup. Season with cayenne pepper and salt. Continue to cook until spinach is heated through.

Spinach and Rice (Spanakorizo)

ngredients

/3 cup olive oil

onions, chopped

pounds fresh spinach, rinsed
nd stemmed

(8 ounce) can tomato sauce

cups water

teaspoon dried dill weed

teaspoon dried parsley

alt and pepper to taste

/2 cup uncooked white rice

Directions

Heat olive oil in a large skillet over medium-high heat. Saute onions in the oil until soft and translucent. Add spinach, and cook stirring for a few minutes, then pour in the tomato sauce and water. Bring to a boil, and season with parsley, dill, salt and pepper. Stir in rice, reduce heat to low, and simmer uncovered for 20 to 25 minutes, or until rice is tender. Add more water if necessary.

Ingredients

1 tablespoon vegetable oil
2 white onions, halved and sliced into 1/2 rings
3 cloves garlic, minced
1/2 cup lentils
2 cups water
1 (10 ounce) package frozen spinach
1 teaspoon salt
1 teaspoon ground cumin
freshly ground black pepper to taste
2 cloves garlic, crushed

Directions

Heat oil in a heavy pan over medium heat. Saute onion for 10 minutes or so, until it begins to turn golden. Add minced garlic and saute for another minute or so.

Add lentils and water to the saucepan. Bring mixture to a boil. Cover, lower heat, and simmer about 35 minutes, until lentils are soft (this may take less time, depending on your water and the lentils).

Meanwhile cook the spinach in microwave according to package directions. Add spinach, salt and cumin to the saucepan. Cover and simmer until all is heated, about ten minutes. Grind in plenty of pepper and press in extra garlic to taste.

Carrot, Tomato, and Spinach Quinoa Pilaf

ngredients

teaspoons olive oil

/2 onion, chopped

cup quinoa

cups water

tablespoons vegetarian chicken-
avored bouillon granules

teaspoon ground black pepper

teaspoon thyme

carrot, chopped

tomato, chopped

cup baby spinach

Directions

Heat the olive oil in a sauce pan over medium heat; cook and stir the onion in the hot oil until translucent, about 5 minutes. Lower the heat, stir in quinoa, and toast, stirring constantly, for 2 minutes. Stir in the water, bouillon granules, black pepper, and thyme; raise heat to high and bring to a boil. Cover, reduce heat to low, and simmer for 5 minutes.

Stir in the carrots. Cover and simmer until all water is absorbed, about 10 more minutes. Turn off the heat, add the tomatoes and spinach, and stir until the spinach is wilted and the tomatoes have given off their moisture, about 2 minutes.

Spinach and Chicken Salad

Ingredients

1 (10 ounce) bag fresh spinach, rinsed and dried
4 cooked skinless, boneless chicken breast halves, sliced
1 zucchini, halved lengthwise and sliced
1 red bell pepper, chopped
1/2 cup black olives
3 ounces fontina cheese, shredded
1/2 cup fat-free roasted garlic salad dressing

Directions

Place equal portions of spinach onto four salad plates. Arrange chicken, zucchini, bell pepper, and black olives over spinach, and top with cheese. Drizzle dressing over salad.

Blackberry Spinach Salad

Ingredients

cups baby spinach, rinsed and dried

pint fresh blackberries

ounces crumbled feta cheese

pint cherry tomatoes, halved

green onion, sliced

/4 cup finely chopped walnuts (optional)

/2 cup edible flowers (optional)

Directions

In a large bowl, toss together baby spinach, blackberries, feta cheese, cherry tomatoes, green onion, and walnuts. Garnish with edible flowers.

Sausage Spinach Manicotti

Ingredients

2 cups shredded mozzarella cheese, divided
1 1/2 cups small curd cottage cheese
1 (10 ounce) package frozen chopped spinach, thawed and squeezed dry
1/2 cup grated Parmesan cheese
1 egg, lightly beaten
1/4 teaspoon dried oregano
1 garlic clove, minced
10 uncooked manicotti shells
1 pound bulk Italian sausage
1 (26 ounce) jar spaghetti sauce
3/4 cup water

Directions

In a large bowl, combine 1 cup mozzarella cheese, cottage cheese, spinach, Parmesan cheese, egg, oregano and garlic; stuff into uncooked manicotti shells. Place in a greased 13-in. x 9-in. x 2-in. baking dish.

Crumble sausage into a large skillet; cook over medium heat until no longer pink. Drain. Stir in spaghetti sauce; pour over manicotti. Pour water along sides of pan. Cover and bake at 350 degrees F for 1 hour. Uncover; sprinkle with remaining mozzarella. Bake 5-8 minutes longer or until cheese is melted. Let stand for 10 minutes before serving.

Delicious Spinach and Turkey Lasagna

ngredients

 whole-wheat lasagna noodles
 teaspoon olive oil
/2 cup chopped onion
 pound ground turkey breast
 cups tomato sauce
/2 cup sliced fresh mushrooms
 tablespoons Italian seasoning
/4 teaspoon ground black
epper
/4 teaspoon garlic powder
 cups chopped fresh spinach
 cups fat-free ricotta cheese
/4 teaspoon ground nutmeg
 cups shredded mozzarella
heese

Directions

Preheat an oven to 375 degrees F (190 degrees C).

Bring a large pot of lightly salted water to a boil. Cook lasagna noodles in boiling water for 8 to 10 minutes. Drain noodles, and rinse with cold water.

Heat the olive oil in a skillet over medium heat. Stir in the onion; cook and stir until the onion has softened and turned translucent, about 2 minutes. Add ground turkey and cook 5 to 7 minutes more, stirring to break up any large chunks of meat. Stir in tomato sauce, mushrooms, Italian seasoning, black pepper, and garlic powder. Simmer for 2 minutes and season to taste.

Combine spinach, ricotta, and nutmeg in a large bowl.

To assemble, arrange 3 noodles lengthwise in the bottom of a greased 9x13 inch baking dish. Spread with 1/3 the ricotta mixture, 1/3 of the turkey mixture, and 1/3 of the mozzarella. Repeat layers, ending with remaining mozzarella. Bake in preheated oven for 25 minutes. Cool for 5 minutes before serving.

Hot Swiss and Spinach Dip with Yogurt

Ingredients

1/2 cup creamy salad dressing, e. g. Miracle Whip в„ў
1/2 cup plain yogurt
1 (10 ounce) package frozen chopped spinach - thawed, drained and squeezed dry
1 (4 ounce) can chopped green chile peppers, drained
1 cup shredded Swiss cheese
3/4 cup grated Parmesan cheese
1 clove garlic, peeled and minced
1/4 teaspoon salt
1/8 teaspoon ground black pepper
1 small tomato, diced

Directions

Preheat oven to 350 degrees F (175 degrees C).

In a medium bowl, mix together creamy salad dressing, plain yogurt, chopped spinach, green chile peppers, Swiss cheese, Parmesan cheese, garlic, salt and ground black pepper.

Transfer the mixture to a 9 inch pie pan. Bake in the preheated oven 25 to 30 minutes, until bubbly and lightly browned. Sprinkle with tomato before serving.

PHILLY Make-Ahead Spinach Phyllo Roll-Ups

ngredients

/2 cup finely chopped green
nions

egg, lightly beaten

(250 g) tub PHILADELPHIA
Cream Cheese Spread

cup KRAFT Feta with Oregano,
Sun Dried Tomatoes and Cracked
Peppercorns

(300 g) package frozen chopped
spinach, thawed, well drained

sheets frozen phyllo pastry,
hawed, divided

/3 cup butter, melted, divided

Directions

Combine all ingredients except phyllo and butter; set aside. Place 1 of the phyllo sheets on clean work surface; brush lightly with butter. Top with 2 more phyllo sheets, brushing more of the remaining butter between each layer. Place remaining phyllo between sheets of plastic wrap; set aside.

Spread one-third of the spinach mixture along one short side of phyllo stack. Fold in ends; roll up to make log. Brush with some of the remaining butter. Repeat with remaining phyllo sheets, spinach mixture and butter. To prevent phyllo from cracking, score logs at 1 inch intervals.

Place in large freezer-weight resealable plastic bags or wrap tightly in plastic wrap until ready to bake. Remove from freezer 30 minutes before baking. Let stand at room temperature while preheating oven to 375 degrees F. Place on baking sheet.

Bake 25 minutes or until golden brown. Cool 5 minutes. Transfer to cutting board. Use serrated knife to cut each log into 10 slices to serve.

Spinach Potatoes Au Gratin

Ingredients

5 cups red potatoes
1/4 cup water
3 tablespoons butter or margarine
1/4 cup chopped onion
1/4 cup all-purpose flour
2 cups milk
1 cup shredded Cheddar cheese
1 teaspoon salt
1 cup chopped fresh spinach
1 tablespoon diced pimientos
4 bacon strips, cooked and crumbled

Directions

In a 2-qt. microwave-safe dish, combine potatoes and water. Cover and microwave on high for 8-9 minutes or until potatoes are tender, stirring twice. Drain; set potatoes aside. In a large microwave-safe bowl, heat butter on high until melted, about 30 seconds. Add onion. Microwave, uncovered, for 1-2 minutes or until tender, stirring once. Whisk in flour until blended. Gradually stir in the milk. Cook, uncovered, on high for 2-1/2 minutes; stir. Cook 3-4 minutes longer, stirring every minute, or until sauce is thickened and bubbly. Stir in cheese and salt. Pour over potatoes. Add spinach and pimientos; mix well. Microwave, uncovered, on high for 2-3 minutes or until heated through, stirring once. Sprinkle with bacon.

Spinach and Mushroom Frittata

Ingredients

egetable cooking spray
0 eggs
 (10.75 ounce) can Campbell's®
:ondensed Cream of Mushroom
oup (Regular or 98% Fat Free)
 (10 ounce) package frozen
pinach, thawed and well drained
 1/2 cups shredded Swiss
heese or Jarlsberg cheese
/2 teaspoon ground black
epper

Directions

Heat the oven to 375 degrees F. Spray a 2-quart shallow baking dish with the cooking spray.

Beat the eggs in a large bowl with a fork or whisk. Stir in the soup. Stir in the spinach, 1 cup cheese and black pepper. Pour the egg mixture into the baking dish.

Bake for 35 minutes or until set. Sprinkle with the remaining cheese.

Ingredients

1/2 cup heavy cream
2 tablespoons unsalted butter
1/2 teaspoon ground nutmeg
1/2 teaspoon salt
ground black pepper to taste
1 pound fresh spinach

Directions

In a medium saucepan over medium heat, mix heavy cream, butter, nutmeg, salt and pepper. Stirring constantly, bring to a boil, then reduce heat to simmer.

Place spinach in a vegetable steamer, and steam until leaves are wilted. Drain in a colander, pressing out excess water with a large spoon.

Coarsely chop spinach in a food processor, and gradually stir into the heavy cream mixture. Briefly return to boiling, then remove from heat.

Cheesy Spinach Casserole

Ingredients

3/4 cup chopped onion

1 tablespoon butter or stick margarine

4 eggs

1 (10 ounce) package frozen chopped spinach, thawed and squeezed dry

2 cups small curd 2% cottage cheese

1 cup shredded reduced-fat Cheddar cheese

3 tablespoons all-purpose flour

1/8 teaspoon salt

Directions

In a small nonstick skillet, saute onion in butter until tender. In large bowl, combine the eggs, egg white and spinach. Stir in the cottage cheese, cheddar cheese, flour, salt and onion mixture. Pour into a 1 -1/2-qt. baking dish coated with nonstick cooking spray. Bake, uncovered, at 350 degrees F for 50-60 minutes or until set.

Gouda and Spinach Stuffed Pork Chops

Ingredients

4 (6 ounce) thick cut pork chops
8 slices smoked Gouda cheese
1/2 pound fresh spinach, rinsed and torn into bite-size pieces
3 tablespoons horseradish mustard
1 cup panko crumbs or breadcrumbs
Creole-style seasoning to taste

Directions

Preheat the oven to 400 degrees F (200 degrees C). Coat a 9x13 inch baking dish with cooking spray.

Lay each chop flat on cutting board, and with a sharp knife held parallel to the board, cut a pocket into the pork, leaving three sides intact. Stuff each chop with spinach, and then with cheese.

Place panko crumbs in a shallow dish. Coat each chop with a thin layer of horseradish, and then roll in crumbs. Arrange chops in prepared baking dish. Sprinkle with Creole seasoning to taste.

Bake in preheated oven for 45 minutes, or until brown and crispy.

Spinach Pecan Bake

Ingredients

medium onion, finely chopped
/4 cup butter or margarine
(10 ounce) packages frozen
spinach, thawed and drained
/2 cup half-and-half cream
/2 cup coarsely chopped pecans
/3 cup dry bread crumbs
teaspoon salt
/2 teaspoon ground nutmeg
/8 teaspoon pepper
TOPPING:
/4 cup dry bread crumbs
tablespoons butter or margarine,
melted

Directions

In a skillet, saute onion in butter until tender. In a large bowl, combine onion, spinach, cream, pecans, bread crumbs, salt, nutmeg and pepper; mix well. Transfer to a greased 1-1/2-qt. baking dish. Combine topping ingredients; sprinkle over the spinachmixture. Bake, uncovered, at 350 degrees F for 30 minutes or until lightly browned.

Spinach Balls

Ingredients

1 (10 ounce) package frozen chopped spinach, thawed and drained
2 cups finely crushed herb-seasoned dry bread stuffing mix
1/2 cup grated Parmesan cheese
2 teaspoons garlic powder
1/2 teaspoon ground black pepper
1 teaspoon Italian seasoning
1/2 cup melted butter
3 eggs, beaten

Directions

Preheat oven to 350 degrees F (175 degrees C).

In a large bowl combine spinach, stuffing mix, Parmesan cheese, garlic powder, black pepper, Italian seasoning, melted butter and eggs. Shape into walnut-sized balls and place on a baking sheet.

Bake in preheated oven for 20 minutes, or until heated through and browned.

Egg and Spinach Casserole

ngredients

eggs, beaten
/4 cup onion, chopped
/4 cup all-purpose flour
 (10 ounce) package frozen
hopped spinach, thawed and
rained
 (16 ounce) package small curd
ottage cheese
 (16 ounce) package shredded
heddar cheese
/2 cup butter, melted
alt and pepper to taste

Directions

Preheat an oven to 350 degrees F (175 degrees C). Prepare a 9x13 inch baking dish with cooking spray.

Beat the eggs in a mixing bowl with the onion and flour until the flour is no longer lumpy. Stir in the spinach, cottage cheese, Cheddar cheese, butter, salt, and pepper until evenly combined; pour into the prepared dish.

Bake in the preheated oven until the casserole is bubbly and the top is golden brown, about 45 minutes.

Spinach Dip

Ingredients

1 (10 ounce) package frozen
chopped spinach, thawed
1 cup minced onion
2 cloves garlic, minced
1 cup minced red bell pepper
1/2 cup sour cream
1/2 cup mayonnaise
1 teaspoon ground cumin
1/2 teaspoon salt

Directions

Squeeze the water out of the spinach, and place the spinach into a
mixing bowl. Stir in the onion, garlic, vegetables, sour cream,
mayonnaise, and cumin. Season with salt and pepper. Let the dip
stand at room temp for 1/2 hour for the flavors to mix, and stir again
before serving. This dip keeps well in the fridge, covered, for up to 1
week.

Spinach with Apples and Pine Nuts

ngredients

tablespoons olive oil
cloves garlic, slivered
tablespoons pine nuts
apple - peeled, cored and
hopped
(10 ounce) bag fresh spinach
alt and black pepper to taste

Directions

Heat the olive oil in a large skillet or wok over low heat. Add the garlic, pine nuts, and apple; cook until the nuts and garlic are golden and the apple is just soft, 3 to 5 minutes.

Increase the heat to medium, and add the spinach to the skillet. Stir and cook another 2 to 3 minutes. Season with salt and pepper to taste.

Greek-Style Shrimp Salad on a Bed of Baby

Ingredients

1 pound raw shrimp (26 to 30 count), peeled
Olive oil to taste
Salt and pepper to taste
Sugar to taste
2 medium tomatoes, cut into medium dice
1/2 cup crumbled feta cheese
1/2 cup pitted and coarsely chopped Kalamata or other black olives
1 teaspoon dried oregano
1/4 cup olive oil
4 teaspoons red wine vinegar
1 (10 ounce) package factory-washed baby spinach leaves

Directions

Thread shrimp onto metal skewers (or bamboo ones that have been soaked in water for 15 minutes). Brush both sides with oil and season with salt, pepper and a light sprinkling of sugar.

Heat gas grill, with all burners on high, until fully preheated, 10 to 15 minutes. Use a wire brush to clean grill rack, then brush lightly with oil. Close lid and allow to return to temperature. Grill shrimp until fully cooked and spotty brown, about 2 minutes per side.

Meanwhile, mix in a medium bowl the tomatoes, cheese, olives, oregano, 2 Tbs. of the olive oil and 2 tsps. of the vinegar. Unthread shrimp and add to bowl. Lightly toss ingredients to coat. Set aside (Can be made an hour or so ahead.)

When ready to serve, drizzle remaining oil, as well as a generous sprinkling of salt and pepper, over spinach in a large bowl. Toss to coat. Add remaining 2 tsps. vinegar; toss again. Divide spinach among 4 large plates. Top with a portion of the shrimp mixture.

Spinach Ziti

Ingredients

8 ounces ziti pasta
1 (14.5 ounce) can Italian-style stewed tomatoes
1/8 teaspoon crushed red pepper flakes
4 ounces fresh spinach, washed and chopped
2 ounces cream cheese
1/4 teaspoon ground nutmeg

Directions

Bring a large pot filled with salted water to a boil. Add ziti and cook until tender but still firm, about 12 minutes.

Meanwhile, in a medium sized non-reactive pan, combine tomatoes and hot pepper flakes. Warm over medium-low heat, breaking up tomatoes if necessary.

Drain pasta and return to hot pan. Add spinach, cream cheese and nutmeg. Cook, stirring, over low heat until spinach wilts, 1-2 minutes. Pour tomato sauce over spinach ziti. Stir and toss gently to mix.

Fresh Spinach and Tarragon Salad

Ingredients

1 bunch spinach, rinsed and torn into bite-size pieces
2 eggs
5 slices bacon
1/2 cup vegetable oil
2 tablespoons red wine vinegar
1 teaspoon white sugar
1/2 teaspoon salt
1/2 teaspoon dried tarragon
1/4 teaspoon ground black pepper

Directions

Place eggs in a saucepan and cover with cold water. Bring water to a boil. Cover, remove from heat, and let eggs stand in hot water for 10 to 12 minutes. Remove from hot water, and cool, peel and chop.

Place bacon in a large, deep skillet. Cook over medium high heat until evenly brown. Drain, crumble and set aside.

Combine the spinach, egg and bacon.

Whisk together the oil, vinegar, sugar, salt, tarragon and pepper. Pour enough dressing over salad to coat; toss and serve.

Easy Spinach Souffle

ngredients

egg
/3 cup 1% milk
/3 cup grated Parmesan cheese
 teaspoon crushed garlic
alt and pepper to taste
 (10 ounce) packages frozen
hopped spinach, thawed and
rained

Directions

Preheat oven to 350 degrees F (175 degrees C).

In a medium bowl whisk together egg, milk, cheese, garlic, salt and pepper. Fold in spinach. Place in a small casserole dish.

Bake in preheated oven for 20 minutes, or until lightly set.

NOTE: If you are in a hurry, use a microwave safe casserole dish, cover with plastic wrap, and cook on high for 3 minutes. Release the steam, recover, and cook on high for another 3 minutes. Enjoy!

Yummy Spinach Dip

Ingredients

1 (10 ounce) package frozen chopped spinach, thawed and drained
1 (16 ounce) container sour cream
3/4 cup mayonnaise
3 green onions, chopped
1 (1 ounce) package dry vegetable dip mix
1 (8 ounce) can water chestnuts, drained and chopped
2 teaspoons prepared Dijon-style mustard

Directions

In a medium bowl, mix together chopped spinach, sour cream, mayonnaise, green onions, dry vegetable dip mix, water chestnuts and prepared Dijon-style mustard. Chill in the refrigerator 8 hours, or overnight, before serving.

Turkey Lasagna with Butternut Squash, Zucchini,

Ingredients

2 tablespoons vegetable oil
1 onion, diced
4 cloves garlic, chopped
1 (20 ounce) package ground turkey
1 (28 ounce) can crushed tomatoes
3 (6 ounce) cans tomato paste
1 1/2 cups water
1 1/2 teaspoons dried basil
1 teaspoon fennel seeds
1 teaspoon Italian seasoning
1/4 teaspoon ground black pepper
1/4 cup chopped fresh parsley
3 1/2 cups peeled and cubed butternut squash
1 (10 ounce) package fresh spinach
1 (15 ounce) container fat-free ricotta cheese
1 egg
2 tablespoons chopped fresh parsley
1/4 teaspoon ground black pepper
1 (6 ounce) package shredded part-skim mozzarella cheese, divided
9 no-boil lasagna noodles
2 zucchini, sliced lengthwise

Directions

Heat the vegetable oil in a large skillet over medium heat; cook the onion and garlic in the hot oil until fragrant, 5 to 7 minutes. Break the turkey into small pieces into the skillet; cook and stir until completely browned, 7 to 10 minutes. Stir the crushed tomatoes, tomato paste, water, basil, fennel seeds, Italian seasoning, 1/4 teaspoon black pepper, and 1/4 cup parsley into the turkey mixture. Reduce heat to medium-low and simmer, stirring occasionally, until the sauce reaches a desired consistency, 60 to 90 minutes.

While the sauce simmers, place the butternut squash in a large, microwave-safe bowl; cover with plastic wrap and cook in microwave on High until tender, about 5 minutes. Set aside.

Cook and stir the spinach in a large skillet over medium heat until wilted, about 5 minutes. Set aside.

Stir the ricotta cheese, egg, 2 tablespoons parsley, 1/4 teaspoon black pepper, and about 2/3 of the mozzarella cheese together in a bowl. Set aside.

Preheat an oven to 375 degrees F (190 degrees C).

Pour 1 1/2 cups of the sauce into the bottom of a 9x13-inch baking dish. Arrange 3 of the lasagna noodles in a layer over the sauce. Spread 1 cup of the ricotta cheese mixture over the noodles. Sprinkle about half of the butternut squash over the ricotta cheese mixture. Layer about half the wilted spinach over the butternut squash. Lay about half the zucchini slices over the spinach in a layer. Repeat the layering. Top with the 3 remaining lasagna noodles. Spread any remaining ricotta cheese mixture over the top of the lasagna. Finish by topping with any remaining sauce mixture. Cover with aluminum foil.

Bake in the preheated oven for 30 minutes. Remove the aluminum foil and sprinkle the remaining mozzarella over the top of the lasagna. Return to oven and bake uncovered until the top is golden brown, about 30 minutes more. Remove and allow the lasagna to rest 15 minutes before cutting to serve.

Japanese Spinach with Sweet Sesame Seeds

Ingredients

2 tablespoons sesame oil
1 tablespoon brown sugar
10 cups fresh spinach leaves
4 tablespoons black sesame seeds, toasted

Directions

Heat the sesame oil in a large skillet over medium heat until hot. Add the spinach 3 to 4 cups at a time. Cook and stir to wilt, then add more spinach.

Grind the sesame seeds into fine crumbs using a mortar and pestle. When spinach is wilted, move it to the sides of the pan and sprinkle sugar in the center. When the sugar melts, stir in the spinach to coat.

Transfer spinach to a serving plate and sprinkle ground sesame seeds on top.

Spinach Lentil Soup

ngredients

cup shredded carrots
large onion, chopped
tablespoon olive oil
cups water
(16 ounce) jar salsa
1/4 cups dried lentils, rinsed
/4 teaspoon salt
(10 ounce) package fresh
pinach, torn

Directions

In a large saucepan or Dutch oven, saute carrots and onion in oil until tender. Add the water, salsa, lentils and salt. Bring to a boil. Reduce heat; cover and simmer for 50-60 minutes or until lentils are tender. Stir in spinach; simmer 5-10 minutes longer or until spinach is wilted.

Spinach and Spaghetti Squash Quiche

Ingredients

1/2 cup frozen chopped spinach , thawed, drained and squeezed dry
1/2 cup cooked, shredded spaghetti squash
1 beaten egg
3 egg whites
1 (12 fluid ounce) can evaporated skim milk
1 cup part-skim-milk mozzarella cheese
cooking spray
1/3 cup bread crumbs

Directions

Preheat oven to 350 degrees F (175 degrees C).

Pierce squash several times with a fork, and place in a microwave-safe dish. Microwave on high for 10 minutes, turn over, and continue cooking 10 minutes more. Squash flesh should be very tender inside. Set aside to cool.

Cut squash in half lengthwise and scoop out seeds. Shred 1/2 cup of squash and place in a mixing bowl. Stir in egg, egg whites, evaporated milk, mozzarella cheese, and spinach until well combined. Spray a 9 inch pie place or quiche dish with cooking spray. Spread bread crumbs in the bottom and around the sides to coat. Pour egg mixture into prepared dish.

Bake quiche in the preheated oven for 45 minutes, or until a toothpick inserted in the center comes out clean. Allow to cool for at least 10 minutes before cutting. Serve warm or at room temperature.

Apple Peanut Spinach Salad

Ingredients

2 (6 ounce) packages fresh baby spinach
1 medium apple, chopped
1/4 cup raisins
2 tablespoons chopped peanuts
2 tablespoons olive oil
1 tablespoon sugar
1 tablespoon cider vinegar
1 tablespoon chutney
3/4 teaspoon curry powder
1/4 teaspoon salt

Directions

In a large bowl, combine the spinach, apple, raisins and peanuts. In a jar with a tight-fitting lid, combine the remaining ingredients; shake well. Drizzle over salad and toss to coat.

Spinach-Stuffed Lamb

Ingredients

3 tablespoons minced garlic
1 tablespoon olive oil
2 (10 ounce) packages frozen chopped spinach, thawed and squeezed dry
8 ounces crumbled goat cheese or feta cheese
3/4 teaspoon salt, divided
1/4 teaspoon pepper, divided
1 (5 pound) boneless butterflied leg of lamb, trimmed
3 cloves garlic, slivered
3 tablespoons minced fresh rosemary

Directions

In a small skillet, saute minced garlic in oil for 2-3 minutes. Remove from the heat; stir in the spinach, cheese, 1/2 teaspoon salt and 1/8 teaspoon pepper.

Untie lamb and open so it lies flat; flatten to 3/4-in. thickness. Spread spinach mixture over meat to within 1 in. of edges. Starting with a short side, roll up lamb and tuck ends in; tie with kitchen string at 2-in. intervals. With a sharp knife, make slits on the outside of meat; insert garlic slivers. Sprinkle with rosemary and remaining salt and pepper.

Place seam side down on a rack in a shallow roasting pan. Cover and bake at 425 degrees F for 1 hour. Uncover; bake 15-30 minutes longer or until browned and a meat thermometer reads 160 degrees F, basting occasionally with pan juices. Let stand for 10-15 minutes before slicing.

Spinach-Stuffed Steak

ngredients

  (10 ounce) package frozen
hopped spinach, thawed and
rained
  (7 ounce) jar roasted red
eppers, drained
  egg white
/2 cup seasoned bread crumbs
/4 cup grated Parmesan cheese
/4 cup sunflower kernels, toasted
  garlic clove, minced
/2 teaspoon salt
  (1 1/2-pound) flank steak

Directions

In a bowl, combine the first eight ingredients; mix well.

Cut steak horizontally from a long edge to within 1/2 in. of opposite
edge; open (like a book) and flatten to 1/2-in. thickness. Spread
spinach mixture over the steak to within 1 in. of edges. Roll up, jelly-
roll style, starting with a long side; tie with kitchen string. Place in a
greased 13-in. x 9-in. x 2-in. baking dish.

Cover and bake at 350 degrees for 1 hour. Uncover; bake 30-45
minutes longer or until tender. Let stand for 10-15 minutes. Cut into
1/2-in. slices.

Spinach Salad with Pepper Jelly Dressing

Ingredients

3 tablespoons mild pepper jelly
2 tablespoons olive oil
1/8 teaspoon salt
1/8 teaspoon Dijon mustard

2 cups baby spinach leaves
2 ounces goat cheese, sliced
2 tablespoons chopped walnuts

Directions

In a small bowl, whisk together the pepper jelly, olive oil, salt and mustard to make the dressing. Heat in the microwave for 30 seconds. Let cool.

Place the spinach in a large bowl, and toss with the dressing. Divide between two serving bowls. Top each one with slices of goat cheese and sprinkle with walnuts.

Spinach Garlic Pasta

Ingredients

- (16 ounce) package angel hair pasta
- cloves garlic, minced
- (10 ounce) package frozen chopped spinach, thawed
- tablespoon olive oil

Directions

Cook the pasta in a large pot of boiling salted water until al dente. Drain.

Heat oil in a large skillet. Add the garlic, and cook for 1 minute. Add the spinach and the cooked pasta. Mix well, and cook for approximately 2 minutes, stirring often. Serve.

Stir-Fry Spinach Salad

Ingredients

1 (8 ounce) can pineapple chunks
1 pound skinless, boneless
chicken breast halves - julienned
2 tablespoons cooking oil
1 medium green pepper, julienned
3 tablespoons brown sugar
1 tablespoon cornstarch
1/4 cup ketchup
3 tablespoons soy sauce
6 cups torn fresh spinach
1 cup cherry tomato halves

Directions

Drain pineapple, reserving 3 tablespoons juice in a small bowl; set pineapple aside. (Discard remaining juice or save for another use.) In a skillet or wok, stir-fry chicken in oil for 5 minutes or until no longer pink. Add green pepper; stir-fry for 2-4 minutes or until crisp-tender. Meanwhile, add brown sugar and cornstarch to pineapple juice; mix well. Stir in ketchup, vinegar and soy sauce until smooth; add to skillet and cook until thickened. On a large serving platter, arrange spinach, pineapple and tomatoes. Top with chicken and green pepper; serve immediately.

Strawberry Spinach Salad I

ngredients

tablespoons sesame seeds
tablespoon poppy seeds
/2 cup white sugar
/2 cup olive oil
/4 cup distilled white vinegar
/4 teaspoon paprika
/4 teaspoon Worcestershire
auce
tablespoon minced onion
0 ounces fresh spinach - rinsed,
ried and torn into bite-size
ieces
quart strawberries - cleaned,
ulled and sliced
/4 cup almonds, blanched and
livered

Directions

In a medium bowl, whisk together the sesame seeds, poppy seeds, sugar, olive oil, vinegar, paprika, Worcestershire sauce and onion. Cover, and chill for one hour.

In a large bowl, combine the spinach, strawberries and almonds. Pour dressing over salad, and toss. Refrigerate 10 to 15 minutes before serving.

Mushroom and Spinach Ravioli with Chive Butter

Ingredients

1 teaspoon olive oil
1 1/2 tablespoons water, or more if needed
2 eggs
2 cups all-purpose flour, or more if needed
1/4 teaspoon salt

1 teaspoon olive oil
1 clove garlic, minced
1/2 cup chopped onion
1 (8 ounce) package fresh mushrooms, coarsely chopped
4 ounces cream cheese, softened
1/3 cup grated Parmesan cheese
1/2 cup mozzarella cheese
1/2 cup frozen chopped spinach, thawed and drained
1 tablespoon chopped fresh chives
1 tablespoon chopped fresh parsley
1/2 teaspoon ground cayenne pepper
salt and ground black pepper to taste
1 egg white, beaten

3 tablespoons butter
1 1/2 teaspoons chopped fresh chives

Directions

Whisk together 1 teaspoon olive oil, water, and whole eggs in a bowl until evenly blended; set aside. Combine flour and salt in a separate large bowl, and make a well in the center. Pour the egg mixture into the well and stir just until combined. Turn dough out onto a lightly floured surface and knead until smooth, 5 to 10 minutes, adding more flour or water as needed. Wrap dough tightly with plastic wrap, and set aside to rest.

Heat 1 teaspoon olive oil in a skillet over medium heat. Stir in the garlic and onion; cook and stir until the onion begins to soften, about 2 minutes. Add the mushrooms, and continue cooking and stirring until the vegetables are soft and the liquid has evaporated, about 10 minutes. Remove from heat, and allow to cool.

Beat cream cheese in a bowl until smooth. Stir in the cooled mushroom mixture, Parmesan cheese, mozzarella cheese, spinach, 1 tablespoon chives, parsley, and cayenne pepper. Season with salt and pepper.

Roll the pasta dough out to about 1/16 inch thick. Cut 3 to 4-inch circles using a large cookie cutter. Roll each circle out as thin as possible. Working with one circle at a time, brush the pasta lightly with the egg white. Scoop about 1 heaping tablespoon full of the mushroom filling onto the center of the pasta, then cover with a second piece of pasta, pinching the edges to seal. Cut the sealed ravioli with the cookie cutter once more to create a uniform shape. Place the finished ravioli on a floured baking sheet, and repeat the process with the remaining pasta and filling.

Fill a large pot with lightly salted water and bring to a rolling boil over high heat. Once the water is boiling, stir in the ravioli and return to a boil. Cook until the pasta floats to the top, 3 to 4 minutes; drain.

To make sauce: Melt butter in a skillet over high heat, cooking and stirring until browned, 5 to 7 minutes. Stir in 1 1/2 teaspoons chives. Serve over hot ravioli.

Spinach, Sausage and Cheese Bake

Ingredients

1 pound Italian sausage
1 (8 ounce) can tomato sauce
2 (10 ounce) packages frozen chopped spinach, thawed and drained
2 cups cottage cheese
1/2 cup grated Parmesan cheese
1 egg, beaten
2 cups shredded mozzarella cheese

Directions

Brown sausage in skillet over medium high heat. Drain fat from skillet and stir in tomato sauce. Set mixture aside.

Preheat oven to 350 degrees F (175 degrees C).

In a large bowl, combine the spinach, cottage cheese, Parmesan cheese and egg. Mix well and spread mixture in the bottom of a 9x13 inch baking dish. Spoon sausage mixture over spinach mixture and top with mozzarella cheese.

Bake in preheated oven for 40 minutes.

Apple-Strawberry Spinach Salad

Ingredients

1 pound fresh spinach, torn
2 cups chopped unpeeled Granny Smith apples
3/4 cup fresh bean sprouts
1/2 cup sliced fresh strawberries
1/4 cup crumbled cooked bacon
DRESSING:
3/4 cup vegetable oil
1/3 cup white wine vinegar
1 small onion, grated
1/2 cup sugar
2 teaspoons Worcestershire sauce
2 teaspoons salt

Directions

In a large salad bowl, combine the first five ingredients. In a small bowl, whisk together all dressing ingredients. Just before serving, pour over salad and toss.

Sweet-Sour Spinach Salad

Ingredients

cup sugar

tablespoon all-purpose flour

/4 teaspoon ground mustard

Dash salt

/3 cup cold water

/3 cup white vinegar

egg, lightly beaten

8 cups fresh spinach, torn

hard-cooked eggs, sliced

/2 pound sliced bacon, cooked and crumbled

slices red onion, separated into rings

Directions

In a small saucepan, combine the sugar, flour, mustard and salt. Gradually stir in water and vinegar until smooth. Bring to a boil; cook and stir for 2 minutes or until thickened. Remove from the heat. Gradually stir a small amount of hot dressing into beaten egg; return all to the pan, stirring constantly. Bring to a gentle boil.

Place spinach in a large salad bowl. Drizzle with warm dressing; toss to coat. Top with the hard-cooked eggs, bacon and onion. Serve immediately.

Spinach-Green Bean Casserole

Ingredients

3/4 cup milk

1 cup sour cream

1 (10.75 ounce) can condensed cream of mushroom soup

2 (15 ounce) cans green beans, drained

1 (14 ounce) can chopped spinach, drained

2 (2.8 ounce) cans French fried onions

Directions

Preheat the oven to 375 degrees F (190 degrees C). Lightly grease a casserole dish.

Stir the milk, sour cream and cream of mushroom soup together in a large bowl. Fold in the green beans and spinach, and mix in about half of the onions. Pour into the casserole dish and top with the remaining onions.

Bake uncovered in the preheated oven until bubbly and browned on top, about 40 minutes.

Greek Pizza with Spinach, Feta and Olives

Ingredients

1/2 cup mayonnaise
4 cloves garlic, minced
1 cup crumbled feta cheese, divided
1 (12 inch) pre-baked Italian pizza crust
1/2 cup oil-packed sun-dried tomatoes, coarsely chopped
1 tablespoon oil from the sun-dried tomatoes
1/4 cup pitted kalamata olives, coarsely chopped
1 teaspoon dried oregano
2 cups baby spinach leaves 1/2 small red onion, halved and thinly sliced

Directions

Adjust oven rack to lowest position, and heat oven to 450 degrees. Mix mayonnaise, garlic and 1/2 cup feta in a small bowl. Place pizza crust on a cookie sheet; spread mayonnaise mixture over pizza, then top with tomatoes, olives and oregano. Bake until heated through and crisp, about 10 minutes.

Toss spinach and onion with the 1 Tb. sun-dried tomato oil. Top hot pizza with spinach mixture and remaining 1/2 cup feta cheese. Return to oven and bake until cheese melts, about 2 minutes longer. Cut into 6 slices and serve.

Belle and Chron's Spinach and Mushroom Quiche

Ingredients

6 slices bacon
4 eggs, beaten
1 1/2 cups light cream
1/4 teaspoon ground nutmeg
1/2 teaspoon salt
1/2 teaspoon pepper
2 cups chopped fresh spinach
2 cups chopped fresh mushrooms
1/2 cup chopped onions
1 cup shredded Swiss cheese
1 cup shredded Cheddar cheese
1 (9 inch) deep dish pie crust

Directions

Preheat oven to 400 degrees F (200 degrees C).

Place bacon in a large, deep skillet. Cook over medium high heat until evenly brown. Drain, crumble and set aside.

In a large bowl, whip together eggs, cream, nutmeg, salt, and pepper. Stir in bacon, spinach, mushrooms, onions, 3/4 cup Swiss cheese, and 3/4 cup Cheddar cheese. Transfer to the pie crust. Top with remaining cheese.

Bake uncovered in the preheated oven 35 minutes, or until bubbly and lightly browned.

Easy Spinach Dip

ngredients

0 slices bacon
 (10 ounce) package frozen
hopped spinach, thawed and
rained
/2 cup salsa
 (8 ounce) package cream
heese
/3 cup chopped green onions
 cup diced tomatoes
/2 cup shredded mozzarella
heese
/4 teaspoon ground cumin
/4 teaspoon salt
/4 teaspoon ground black
epper
/4 teaspoon garlic powder

Directions

Place bacon in a large, deep skillet. Cook over medium high heat until evenly brown. Drain, crumble and set aside.

In a medium saucepan over medium heat, cook and stir the spinach, salsa, cream cheese and green onions until the cream cheese has melted. Mix in the crumbled bacon and tomatoes. Remove from heat. Mix in the mozzarella cheese, cumin, salt, pepper and garlic powder.

Chicken Spinach Quiche

Ingredients

1 cup shredded Cheddar cheese, divided
1 (9 inch) unbaked pastry shell
1 cup diced cooked chicken
1 (10 ounce) package frozen chopped spinach, thawed and squeezed dry
1/4 cup finely chopped onion
2 eggs
3/4 cup milk
3/4 cup mayonnaise*
1/4 teaspoon salt
1/8 teaspoon pepper

Directions

Sprinkle 1/4 cup cheese into the pastry shell. In a bowl, combine the chicken, 1/2 cup spinach, onion and remaining cheese (save remaining spinach for another use). Spoon into pastry shell. in a bowl, whisk the eggs, milk, mayonnaise, salt and pepper; pour over the chicken mixture.

Bake at 350 degrees F for 40-45 minutes or until a knife inserted near the center comes out clean. Let stand for 15 minutes before cutting.

Holiday Hot Spinach Dip

Ingredients

1 (10 ounce) package frozen chopped spinach, thawed and drained
1/2 cup red bell pepper, diced
1 tablespoon minced garlic
1 (6.5 ounce) jar artichoke hearts, drained and mashed
1/2 cup sour cream
1/2 cup grated Parmesan cheese
salt and ground black pepper to taste
1/4 cup heavy cream

Directions

Preheat oven to 350 degrees F (175 degrees C).

Mix together spinach, bell pepper, garlic, artichokes, sour cream, and parmesan cheese. Season with salt and pepper. Mixture will be thick, add cream to thin to dip consistency. Spoon into a 1 quart baking dish.

Bake for 20 minutes, or until bubbly. Serve with crackers.

Make-Ahead PHILLY Spinach Phyllo Roll-Ups

Ingredients

1/2 cup finely chopped green onions
1 egg, beaten
1 (250 g) tub PHILADELPHIA Cream Cheese Spread
1 cup KRAFT Feta with Oregano, Sun Dried Tomatoes and Cracked Peppercorns Cheese
1 (300 g) package frozen chopped spinach, thawed, well drained
15 sheets frozen phyllo dough, thawed, divided
1/3 cup butter, melted, divided

Directions

Combine all ingredients except phyllo and butter. Place 1 phyllo sheet on clean work surface; brush lightly with butter. Top with 2 more phyllo sheets, brushing some of the remaining butter between each layer. Place remaining phyllo between sheets of plastic wrap; set aside.

Spread 1/5 of the spinach mixture along one short side of phyllo stack to within 1 inch of ends. Fold in long sides of phyllo; roll up from one short side to make log. Brush with some of the remaining butter. Repeat with remaining phyllo sheets, spinach mixture and butter. To prevent phyllo from cracking, score logs at 1-inch intervals.

Place in large freezer-weight resealable plastic bags. (Or wrap tightly in plastic wrap until ready to bake.) Remove from freezer 30 minutes before baking. Let stand at room temperature while heating oven to 375 degrees F. Place on baking sheet.

Bake 25 minutes or until golden brown. Cool 5 minutes. Transfer to cutting board. Use serrated knife to cut each log into 6 slices to serve.

Spinach Sole Roll-Ups

Ingredients

 (10 ounce) package frozen leaf spinach, thawed and squeezed dry
/2 cup sliced green onions
/3 cup sour cream
 1/4 pounds sole fillets
emon-pepper seasoning
 tablespoon cornstarch
 tablespoon water
 (14.5 ounce) can stewed omatoes, undrained

Directions

In a small bowl, combine the spinach, onions and sour cream. Spread into an ungreased 13-in. x 9-in. x 2-in. baking dish. Cut sole fillets into 6-in. x 2-in. strips; carefully roll up and secure with toothpicks. Place over spinach mixture. Sprinkle with lemon-pepper. Bake, uncovered, at 350 degrees F for 15-20 minutes or until fish flakes easily with a fork.

In a saucepan, combine cornstarch and water until smooth. Gradually add tomatoes. Bring to a boil over medium heat; cook and stir for 2 minutes or until thickened. Discard toothpicks from roll-ups. Spoon tomato sauce over roll-ups and spinach mixture.

Byrdhouse Spinach Soup

Ingredients

1/4 cup butter
1/4 cup flour
1 (8 ounce) package sliced mushrooms
1/2 cup dry sherry
1 (14.5 ounce) can chicken broth
1 quart milk
2 bunches fresh spinach, cleaned and chopped
4 green onions, chopped 1/2 teaspoon ground nutmeg salt and pepper to taste
8 ounces cooked small shrimp

Directions

Melt butter in a large saucepan over medium heat. Whisk in flour, and cook until the mixture turns a darker yellow color, about 5 minutes. Stir in the mushrooms, and cook for 2 minutes.

Whisk in the sherry, chicken broth, and milk, then add the spinach, green onion, nutmeg, salt, and pepper. Bring to a boil over high heat, whisking constantly, then reduce heat to medium low, and simmer until the spinach is tender, 15 to 20 minutes. Garnish with shrimp to serve.

Cumin Lamb Steaks with Smashed Potatoes,

Ingredients

20 new potatoes, halved
1 tablespoon butter
2 cloves garlic, minced
2 tablespoons brown sugar
1 cup red wine

4 (6 ounce) lamb shoulder steaks
salt and pepper to taste
1 tablespoon cumin seeds
1 tablespoon vegetable oil

2 bunches fresh spinach, cleaned
1/4 cup sour cream
2 tablespoons softened butter

Directions

Place potatoes into a large saucepan and cover with salted water. Bring to a boil, then reduce heat to medium-low, cover, and simmer until tender, about 15 minutes. Drain and allow to steam dry for a minute or two.

Melt the butter in a saucepan over medium heat. Stir in the garlic, and cook for 3 to 4 minutes until the aroma of the garlic has mellowed. Add the brown sugar and red wine, then bring to a boil over medium-high heat. Allow to boil for 5 minutes, then remove from the heat, cover, and keep warm.

Meanwhile, season the lamb steaks with salt and pepper to taste. Press the cumin seeds into the steaks on both sides. Heat the vegetable oil in a large skillet over medium-high heat. Add the steaks, and cook on both sides until cooked to your desired degree of doneness, about 4 minutes per side for medium. Remove the steaks to rest in a warm spot. Place the spinach into the hot skillet, season to taste with salt and pepper, and cook until the spinach has wilted.

Mash the potatoes with the sour cream and butter; season to taste with salt and pepper. To serve, mound a serving of mashed potatoes onto the center of a dinner plate. Top with the spinach and a lamb steak. Strain the red wine sauce overtop.

Spinach Manicotti

Ingredients

1 (15 ounce) container nonfat ricotta cheese
2 cups shredded part-skim mozzarella cheese, divided
1 (10 ounce) package frozen chopped spinach, thawed and squeezed dry
1/2 cup reduced-fat sour cream
1/4 cup dry bread crumbs
1 tablespoon Italian seasoning
1 teaspoon garlic powder
1 teaspoon onion powder
2 cups tomato juice
1 cup chunky salsa
1 (15 ounce) can crushed tomatoes
14 uncooked manicotti shells

Directions

In a large bowl, combine the ricotta, 1-1/2 cups mozzarella cheese, spinach, sour cream, bread crumbs, Italian seasoning, garlic powder and onion powder. Combine the tomato juice, salsa and crushed tomatoes; spread 1 cup sauce in a ungreased 13-in. x 9-in. x 2-in. baking dish. Stuff uncooked manicotti with spinach mixture; arrange over sauce. Pour remaining sauce over manicotti.

Cover and bake at 350 degrees F for 55 minutes. Uncover; sprinkle with remaining mozzarella cheese. Bake 15 minutes longer or until noodles are tender.

Best Ever Spinach Artichoke Dip

ngredients

(10 ounce) package frozen
hopped spinach, thawed and
rained
(14 ounce) can artichoke hearts,
rained and chopped
cup shredded Italian cheese
lend
/2 cup mayonnaise
cup Alfredo sauce

Directions

Preheat oven to 350 degrees F (175 degrees C).

In a small casserole dish, mix the spinach, artichoke hearts, cheese, mayonnaise, and Alfredo sauce.

Bake 20 minutes in the preheated oven, or until lightly bubbly and lightly browned.

Spinach Mushroom Quiche

Ingredients

2 tablespoons butter
2 cups fresh sliced mushrooms
2 cups torn spinach leaves
6 green onions, chopped
1 (8 ounce) package refrigerated crescent rolls
1 (1 ounce) package herb and lemon soup mix
1/2 cup half-and-half
4 eggs, beaten
1 cup shredded Monterey Jack cheese

Directions

Preheat oven to 375 degrees F (190 degrees C).

Melt margarine in a skillet over medium heat and cook mushrooms, spinach and onions for 5 minutes or until tender, stir continuously. Remove the skillet from heat.

In a 9 inch round pan or pie plate coated with non-stick cooking spray arrange crescent roll triangles in a circle, with narrow tips hung over the rim of the pie plate about 2 inches. Press dough onto the bottom and side of the pie plate to fill in any gaps.

In a medium bowl stir together the soup mix, half and half cream and eggs. Stir the cheese and cooked vegetables into the egg mixture until blended. Pour into the prepared crust. Fold the points of dough that are hanging over the edge back in over the filling.

Bake the quiche for 30 minutes in the preheated oven, or until a knife inserted into the center comes out clean.

Pan Seared Sea Bass with Warm Spinach Salad

Ingredients

1/4 cup CRISCO® Canola Oil*, divided
4 (6 ounce) fillets sea bass
Salt and pepper to taste
1 red onion, cut into thin strips
2 cups button mushrooms, sliced
1 tomato, cut into 8 wedges
1 pound fresh baby spinach, stems removed
4 slices crisply cooked bacon, chopped
3 tablespoons sunflower seeds
1 tablespoon balsamic vinegar

Directions

In a large heavy skillet heat 2 tablespoons CRISCO® Oil over medium-high heat, until hot but not smoking. Sprinkle fillets with salt and pepper. Cook on one side, about 7 minutes, or until golden brown. Carefully turn each fillet; cook 5 minutes more. Remove from the pan and set aside.

Add the remaining CRISCO® Oil to the pan. Add onions, mushrooms, tomato, spinach, bacon and sunflower seeds; saute quickly over medium-high heat. Add vinegar; toss and cook just until warm. Place spinach mixture on 4 serving plates; top each with a sea bass fillet.

Hot Spinach and Artichoke Salad

Ingredients

1 tablespoon olive oil
1 (10 ounce) package spinach - rinsed, stemmed, and dried
1 red onion, thinly sliced
1 (8 ounce) jar marinated artichoke hearts
1 cup crumbled feta cheese

Directions

Preheat oven to 300 degrees F (150 degrees C).

Drizzle olive oil on a rimmed baking sheet. Spread spinach leaves in a thick layer covering the baking sheet. Arrange onions and artichokes over the spinach, and drizzle the marinade from the jar over the entire salad. Sprinkle with the cheese (and sausage, if you wish).

Bake for about 10 minutes, or until the spinach is wilted but NOT crispy.

Spinach and Artichoke Dip

Ingredients

(14 ounce) can artichoke hearts, drained and chopped

(10 ounce) package frozen chopped spinach, thawed and drained

cup mayonnaise

cup grated Parmesan cheese

1/2 cups shredded Monterey Jack cheese

Directions

Preheat oven to 350 degrees F (175 degrees C). Lightly grease a 1 quart baking dish.

In a medium bowl, mix together artichoke hearts, spinach, mayonnaise, Parmesan cheese and 2 cups Monterey Jack cheese. Transfer mixture to the prepared baking dish, and sprinkle with remaining 1/2 cup of Monterey Jack cheese.

Bake in the center of the preheated oven until the cheese is melted, about 15 minutes.

Ingredients

1 (10 ounce) package pre-washed fresh spinach
1 cup fresh green peas
1/4 cup olive oil
1 1/2 lemons, juiced
1/4 cup crumbled feta cheese
salt and pepper to taste

Directions

In a large bowl, toss together the spinach, peas and olive oil until evenly coated. Add the lemon juice, feta and salt and pepper, and toss again.

Parsley Spinach Chicken Stew

Ingredients

1 cup chopped fresh parsley
8 ounces spinach, rinsed and chopped
1 onion, chopped
1 potato, cubed
4 skinless, boneless chicken breasts
6 tablespoons olive oil
1/4 teaspoon salt
1/4 teaspoon ground turmeric
2 tablespoons tomato paste
1 cup water
3 tablespoons fresh lemon juice

Directions

In a medium size frying pan, heat 4 tablespoons of the olive oil. Add the parsley and spinach and fry until wilted. Set aside.

Heat the other 2 tablespoons of olive oil in a large pot. Add the onion and saute, stirring occasionally, until tender. Add the chicken breasts and brown both sides of each breast. Add the salt, turmeric, fried parsley/spinach, water and tomato paste. Bring all to a boil and let boil for 10 minutes.

Add the cubed potatoes. Cover and let cook over low heat for 1 to 2 hours. Add the lemon juice, bring to a boil and let boil for 10 more minutes. Serve with steamed rice if desired.

Spinach and Tortellini Salad

Ingredients

1 (9 ounce) package cheese-filled tortellini
1 (10 ounce) package frozen chopped spinach, thawed and drained
1/3 cup grated Parmesan cheese
2 cups cherry tomatoes, halved
1 (2 ounce) can sliced black olives
1 (8 ounce) bottle Italian-style salad dressing

Directions

In a large pot of salted boiling water, cook pasta until al dente, rinse under cold water and drain.

In a large bowl, combine the tortellini, spinach, cheese, tomatoes and olives. Add enough salad dressing to coat. Toss and season with salt and pepper.

Spinach Artichoke Pie

ngredients

 tablespoons vegetable oil, ivided
/4 cup dry bread crumbs
/2 pound fresh mushrooms, liced
 pound fresh spinach, chopped nd cooked
 (6.5 ounce) jar marinated rtichoke hearts, drained and uartered
 cup day-old bread cubes
 1/4 cups shredded Cheddar heese, divided
 (4 ounce) jar diced pimientos, rained
 eggs, beaten
/4 teaspoon garlic powder

Directions

Brush the bottom and sides of a 9-in. pie plate with 2 tablespoons oil; sprinkle with bread crumbs. Set aside.

In a skillet, saute mushrooms in remaining oil; drain. Remove from the heat. Squeeze spinach dry; add to mushrooms. Stir in artichokes, bread cubes, 1 cup of cheese, pimientos, eggs and garlic powder; stir well.

Spoon into the prepared pie plate. Bake, uncovered, at 350 degrees F for 30 minutes. Sprinkle with remaining cheese. Bake 5-10 minutes longer or until the cheese is melted. Let stand for 10 minutes before cutting.

Easy Spinach Lasagna with White Sauce

Ingredients

1 (10 ounce) package frozen chopped spinach
29 ounces Alfredo-style pasta sauce
1/2 cup skim milk
1 (8 ounce) package lasagna noodles
1 pint part-skim ricotta cheese 1 egg
8 ounces shredded carrots
8 ounces fresh mushrooms, sliced
1/2 cup shredded mozzarella cheese

Directions

Preheat oven to 350 degrees F (175 degrees C). Coat a 10x15 inch lasagna pan with cooking spray.

Place the spinach in a medium bowl. Microwave, uncovered, on high for 4 minutes. Mix in ricotta. Beat the egg with a wire whisk, and add it to the spinach and ricotta. Stir well to blend.

Combine pasta sauce with milk in a medium bowl. Mix well.

Spread about 1/2 cup pasta sauce mixture evenly in the bottom of the dish. Place 3 uncooked noodles over the sauce. Spread half of the spinach mixture over the noodles. Sprinkle with half of the carrots and half of the mushrooms. Place 3 more noodles over the vegetable mixture. Pour 1 1/2 cups sauce over the noodles.
Spread the remaining spinach mixture over the sauce, followed by layers of the remaining carrots and mushrooms. Place 3 more noodles over the vegetables. Pour remaining sauce evenly on top Sprinkle with the mozzarella cheese. Spray a sheet of aluminum foi with cooking spray. Cover the dish tightly with aluminum foil, spray side down.

Bake for 50 to 60 minutes. Remove from oven, uncover, and spoor some sauce over the exposed top noodles. Turn the oven off, and place the uncovered dish back into the warm oven for 15 more minutes. Serve at once, or let rest until ready to serve.

Rice with Lemon and Spinach

ngredients

small onion, chopped
cup sliced fresh mushrooms
garlic cloves, minced
tablespoon olive oil
cups cooked long-grain rice
(10 ounce) package frozen
chopped spinach, thawed and
squeezed dry
tablespoons lemon juice
1/2 teaspoon salt
1/4 teaspoon dill weed
1/8 teaspoon pepper
1/3 cup crumbled feta cheese,
divided

Directions

In a skillet, saute the onion, mushrooms and garlic in oil until tender. Stir in the rice, spinach, lemon juice, salt, dill and pepper. Reserve 1 tablespoon cheese. Stir remaining into skillet; mix well.

Transfer to an 8-in. square baking dish coated with nonstick cooking spray. Sprinkle with reserved cheese. Cover and bake at 350 degrees F for 25 minutes. Uncover; bake 5-10 minutes longer or until heated through and cheese is melted.

Passover Spinach Fritatta

Ingredients

2 (10 ounce) packages frozen
chopped spinach
3 matzo crackers
4 eggs, beaten
salt and pepper to taste
1 pinch ground nutmeg
3 tablespoons butter
2 tablespoons grated Parmesan
cheese

Directions

Heat the spinach in a saucepan with 1/2 cup of water, until
completely thawed. Strain the spinach, reserving half the amount of
liquid.

Crumble the matzo into a medium-size mixing bowl and pour the
spinach and the remaining liquid over them. Mix thoroughly until the
matzo are softened. Add the Parmesan, eggs, salt, nutmeg and
pepper.

Heat the margarine in a 12 inch skillet and add the spinach mixture.
Cook on medium heat, uncovered for 5 minutes on each side.
Sprinkle with grated Parmesan and serve immediately.

Simple Cranberry Spinach Salad

Ingredients

(6 ounce) package fresh spinach
/3 cup dried cranberries
/3 cup chopped walnuts
/3 cup raspberry walnut
inaigrette
tablespoon finely shredded
Romano cheese

Directions

Combine the spinach, cranberries, walnuts, vinaigrette, and Romano cheese in a large bowl; toss until spinach is evenly coated. Serve immediately.

Spinach Brownies

Ingredients

1 (10 ounce) package spinach, rinsed and chopped
1 cup all-purpose flour
1 teaspoon salt
1 teaspoon baking powder
2 eggs
1 cup milk
1/2 cup butter, melted
1 onion, chopped
1 (8 ounce) package shredded mozzarella cheese

Directions

Preheat oven to 375 degrees F (190 degrees C). Lightly grease a 9x13 inch baking dish.

Place spinach in a medium saucepan with enough water to cover Bring to a boil. Lower heat to simmer and cook until spinach is limp about 3 minutes. Remove from heat and set aside.

In a large bowl, mix flour, salt and baking powder. Stir in eggs, milk and butter. Mix in spinach, onion and mozzarella cheese.

Transfer the mixture to the prepared baking dish. Bake in the preheated oven 30 to 35 minutes, or until a toothpick inserted in the center comes out clean. Cool before serving.

Spinach Lasagna III

ngredients

0 lasagna noodles
! tablespoons olive oil
 cup chopped fresh mushrooms
 cup chopped onion
 tablespoon minced garlic
! cups fresh spinach
 cups ricotta cheese
!/3 cup grated Romano cheese
 teaspoon salt
 teaspoon dried oregano
 teaspoon dried basil leaves
/2 teaspoon ground black
epper
 egg
 cups shredded mozzarella
heese
 cups tomato pasta sauce
 cup grated Parmesan cheese

Directions

Preheat oven to 350 degrees F (175 degrees C).

Bring a large pot of lightly salted water to a boil. Add lasagna noodles and cook for 8 to 10 minutes or until al dente; drain.

In a skillet over medium-high heat, cook mushrooms, onions, and garlic in olive oil until onions are tender. Drain excess liquid and cool. Boil spinach for 5 minutes. Drain, then squeeze out excess liquid. Chop spinach.

Combine ricotta cheese, Romano cheese, spinach, salt, oregano, basil, pepper, and egg in a bowl. Add cooled mushroom mixture. Beat with an electric mixer on low speed for 1 minute. Lay 5 lasagna noodles in bottom of a 9x13 inch baking dish. Spread one third of the cheese/spinach mixture over noodles. Sprinkle 1 cup mozzarella cheese and 1/3 cup Parmesan cheese on top. Spread 1 cup spaghetti sauce over cheese. Repeat layering 2 times.

Cover dish with aluminum foil and bake in a preheated oven for 1 hour. Cool 15 minutes before serving.

Spinach Pie

Ingredients

2 pounds spinach, rinsed and chopped
8 ounces feta cheese, crumbled
1 (8 ounce) container cottage cheese
1/2 cup chopped onion
3/4 teaspoon poultry seasoning
2 teaspoons chopped fresh dill
1/4 teaspoon ground black pepper
salt to taste
2 cups bread crumbs
4 tablespoons butter, melted

Directions

Preheat oven to 350 degrees F (175 degrees C). Lightly grease one 9x13 inch casserole dish.

In a large bowl, combine the spinach, feta cheese, cottage cheese, onion, poultry seasoning, dill, pepper and salt. Mix well and pour into prepared dish.

Mix together the breadcrumbs and butter. Sprinkle over spinach mixture and bake at 350 degrees F (175 degrees C) for 30 minutes.

Spinach Stuffing Balls

Ingredients

eggs, lightly beaten
(6 ounce) package stuffing mix
/2 cup butter or margarine,
melted
cup grated Parmesan cheese
/4 teaspoon salt
/8 teaspoon pepper
(10 ounce) packages frozen
chopped spinach, thawed and
squeezed dry

Directions

In a bowl, combine eggs, stuffing mix, butter, Parmesan cheese, salt and pepper. Add spinach; mix well. Shape into 1-1/2-in. balls; place in an ungreased 15-in. x 10-in. x 1-in. baking pan. Bake at 350 degrees F for 12-15 minutes or until lightly browned.

Syrian-Style Lentil and Spinach Soup

Ingredients

1 tablespoon olive oil
1 onion, chopped
2/3 cup dry green lentils
1 3/4 cups water
1 tablespoon all-purpose flour
2/3 cup chopped fresh spinach
3 tablespoons lemon juice
1/2 teaspoon salt

Directions

Heat oil in a pot over medium heat. Stir in onion and cook until soft, about 7 minutes, stirring occasionally. Add the lentils and water and bring to a boil, then reduce heat to low and simmer, uncovered, until lentils are tender, 20 to 25 minutes. Cooking times will vary depending on the freshness of the lentils.

Ladle a half cup of the soup liquid into a bowl and whisk in the flour to form a paste. Mix the paste into the soup. Add the spinach, lemon juice, and salt. If you prefer a thinner soup, add a bit more water. Cook until spinach is wilted, about 5 minutes. Adjust salt and lemon to suit your taste.

Spinach Phyllo Cups

ngredients

egg, beaten
! cloves garlic, finely minced
 (8 ounce) package crumbled
eta cheese
! (10 ounce) boxes frozen
:hopped spinach, thawed and
;queezed dry
 (2.1 ounce) packages pre-baked
nini phyllo dough shells

Directions

Preheat oven to 400 degrees F (200 degrees C).

Mix the egg, garlic, and feta in a large bowl. Stir in the spinach.
Place the phyllo shells on flat baking sheets, and fill with the
spinach mixture.

Bake in preheated oven until hot, 6 to 8 minutes.

Makeover Garlic Spinach Balls

Ingredients

2 cups crushed seasoned stuffing
1 cup finely chopped onion
3/4 cup egg substitute
1 egg, lightly beaten
1/4 cup grated Parmesan cheese
1/4 cup butter, melted
3 tablespoons reduced sodium chicken or vegetable broth
1 garlic clove, minced
1 1/2 teaspoons dried thyme
1/4 teaspoon pepper
1/8 teaspoon salt
2 (10 ounce) packages frozen chopped spinach, thawed and squeezed dry

Directions

In a large bowl, combine the first 11 ingredients. Stir in spinach until blended. Roll into 1-in. balls. Place in a 15-in. x 10-in. x 1-in. baking pan coated with nonstick cooking spray. Bake at 350 degrees F for 15-20 minutes or until golden brown.

Mostaccioli with Spinach and Feta

Ingredients

ounces penne pasta
tablespoons olive oil
cups chopped tomatoes
0 ounces fresh spinach, washed
nd chopped
clove garlic, minced
ounces tomato basil feta cheese
alt to taste
round black pepper to taste

Directions

Cook pasta according to package directions. Drain, and set aside.

Heat oil in a large pot. Add tomatoes, spinach, and garlic; cook and stir 2 minutes, or until spinach is wilted and mixture is thoroughly heated. Add pasta and cheese; cook 1 minute. Season to taste with salt and pepper.

Sesame Strawberry Spinach Salad

Ingredients

1/2 cup SPLENDA® No Calorie
Sweetener, Granulated
2 tablespoons sesame seeds
1/2 teaspoon sesame oil
1 tablespoon poppy seeds
1 1/2 teaspoons dried minced
onion
1/4 teaspoon paprika
1/2 cup vegetable oil
1/2 cup balsamic vinegar
2 bunches fresh spinach -
chopped, washed and dried
1 pint strawberries, halved

Directions

Whisk together the SPLENDA® Granulated Sweetener, sesame seeds, sesame oil, poppy seeds, dried onion, paprika, oil and vinegar. Refrigerate until chilled.

In a salad bowl, combine the spinach and strawberries. Drizzle with dressing, toss lightly and serve.

Spinach and Yogurt Soup

ngredients

1/2 tablespoons butter or
nargarine
medium onion, finely chopped
teaspoons all-purpose flour
/3 teaspoon salt
/4 teaspoon dried tarragon
pinch ground nutmeg
pinch cayenne pepper
(16 ounce) package frozen
chopped spinach, thawed
cups chicken broth
/4 cup plain yogurt
slices lemon, cut in half for
garnish

Directions

Melt butter in a large saucepan over medium heat. Add the onion, and cook until tender, stirring occasionally. Stir in the flour, salt, tarragon, nutmeg and cayenne, and heat until fragrant. Stir in spinach (undrained) and chicken broth. Bring to a boil, then reduce heat to low, and simmer for about 15 minutes.

Remove the soup from the heat, and puree in a food processor or blender in batches. Return to the saucepan, and whisk in yogurt. Heat through, but do not boil. Taste and adjust seasonings if necessary. Ladle into bowls, and float a lemon slice on top of each serving.

Wilted Spinach Salad

Ingredients

6 eggs
1 pound bacon
2 bunches fresh spinach, rinsed and dried
4 green onions, thinly sliced
2 eggs
1/4 cup white sugar
1/4 cup white vinegar
1/4 cup red wine vinegar

Directions

Place 6 eggs in a medium saucepan with enough cold water to cover. Bring water to a boil, and immediately remove from heat. Cover, and let eggs stand in hot water for 10 to 12 minutes. Remove from hot water, cool, peel, and chop.

Place bacon in a large, deep skillet. Cook over medium high heat until evenly brown. Drain, crumble, and set aside, reserving approximately 1/2 cup of drippings in the skillet.

In a large bowl, toss together the spinach and green onions.

Heat the reserved drippings over low heat. In a small bowl, whisk together the 2 remaining eggs, sugar, white vinegar, and red wine vinegar. Add to warm grease, and whisk for about a minute, until thickened. Pour at once over spinach, add crumbled bacon, and toss to coat. Garnish with chopped egg.

Tahini Spinach

Ingredients

(10 ounce) package frozen
chopped spinach
/2 cup water
tablespoon tahini
cloves garlic, minced
/4 teaspoon ground cumin
/4 teaspoon paprika
cayenne pepper, or to taste
/3 cup red wine vinegar
salt and pepper to taste

Directions

Place the spinach and water into a saucepan, and bring to a boil over high heat. Reduce heat to medium-low, cover, and simmer 4 to 6 minutes until tender.

Meanwhile, whisk together the tahini, garlic, cumin, paprika, cayenne pepper, and red wine vinegar. Season to taste with salt and pepper. Drain the cooked spinach, and top with the tahini sauce to serve.

Ingredients

1 1/2 pounds boneless chicken breast
1 cup Newman's OwnB® Teriyaki Marinade
1 (3 ounce) package ramen noodles
1/2 cup slivered almonds
1 teaspoon sesame seeds
1 tablespoon sesame oil
2 bunches baby spinach
3 scallions
8 ounces Mandarin oranges
1/3 cup Newman's OwnB® Lighten UpB® Low Fat Sesame Ginger Dressing

Directions

Clean and trim chicken. Place in bowl with 1 cup marinade. Cover and refrigerate for an hour or longer.

Remove from bowl, discard marinade and grill or saute over medium heat, approximately 7 minutes each side. Set aside, let cool, then shred into small pieces with two forks.

In medium saute pan over medium heat add sesame oil. Crumble ramen noodles and add to pan along with almond slices and sesame seeds. Lightly brown and remove from heat.

Wash and dry baby spinach and place in a large bowl. Thinly slice scallions and add to spinach. Add Mandarin oranges and shredded chicken.

Drizzle salad with Sesame Ginger Dressing to taste, toss, and serve.

Spinach Crescents

Ingredients

/2 cup sliced almonds

(10 ounce) package frozen
chopped spinach, thawed and
squeezed dry

/2 cup grated Parmesan cheese

/4 cup chopped onion

2 teaspoons olive or vegetable oil

/4 teaspoon salt

/8 teaspoon pepper

(8 ounce) package refrigerated
crescent rolls

Directions

In a food processor or blender, finely chop the almonds. Add spinach, Parmesan cheese, onion, oil, salt and pepper; cover and process until well blended. Unroll and separate the crescent dough into eight pieces. Spread spinach mixture evenly over dough to within 1/8 in. of edges. Roll up and place on a greased baking sheet. Bake at 375 degrees F for 15-18 minutes or until golden brown. Serve warm.

Ingredients

2 (10 ounce) packages frozen chopped spinach
1 (10.75 ounce) can condensed cream of mushroom soup
1 tablespoon butter
garlic salt to taste

Directions

Prepare spinach according to package directions; drain well.

In a large saucepan over medium-high heat, combine spinach, mushroom soup and butter. Bring to a low boil. Season with garlic salt to taste.

Spinach Wild Rice Quiche

Ingredients

(9 inch) unbaked pastry shell
eggs
cup half-and-half cream
cup vegetable wild rice or
ooked wild rice
cup shredded Swiss cheese
bacon strips, cooked and
rumbled
/2 cup frozen chopped spinach,
hawed

Directions

Line unpricked pastry shell with a double thickness of heavy-duty foil. Bake at 450 degrees F for 5 minutes. Remove foil; bake 5 minutes longer. Remove from the oven; reduce heat to 350 degrees F.

In a bowl, beat the eggs and cream. Add rice, cheese, bacon and spinach; mix well. Pour into prepared crust. Cover edges of pastry with foil. Bake for 30-35 minutes or until a knife inserted near the center comes out clean.

Pumpernickel Spinach Dip I

Ingredients

1 (8 ounce) container sour cream
1/2 (8 ounce) package cream
cheese, softened
2 tablespoons mayonnaise
1 (1 ounce) package dry dill dip
mix
1/2 bunch spinach, rinsed and
chopped
1 (8 ounce) loaf round
pumpernickel loaf

Directions

In a medium bowl, stir together the sour cream, cream cheese, mayonnaise, dill dip mix and spinach.

Cut out the center of the pumpernickel loaf, creating a bowl. Cut the removed bread into bite-sized pieces. Fill the hollowed loaf with the sour cream mixture. Serve with the bread pieces.

Yogurt Spinach Dip

Ingredients

cup chopped fresh spinach
cup plain yogurt
cup mayonnaise
teaspoons seasoning salt
/4 teaspoon dried parsley
/4 teaspoon dried basil
/4 teaspoon dried oregano 1/4
easpoon ground dry mustard 1/4
easpoon garlic salt

Directions

In a medium bowl, mix together spinach, plain yogurt, mayonnaise, seasoning salt, parsley, basil, oregano, dry mustard and garlic salt. Chill until serving.

Spinach Chicken Pockets

Ingredients

3/4 pound skinless, boneless chicken breast halves
1/2 cup reduced-fat plain yogurt
2 tablespoons reduced-fat mayonnaise
1 tablespoon Dijon mustard
1/4 teaspoon ground cumin
1/8 teaspoon cayenne pepper
2 cups fresh baby spinach
1/2 cup chopped seeded cucumber
2 green onions, sliced
4 (6-inch) pita breads, halved

Directions

In a large nonstick skillet coated with nonstick cooking spray, cook chicken over medium heat for 10-12 minutes on each side or until juices run clear. Remove; thinly sliced chicken and cool.

Meanwhile, in a small bowl, combine the yogurt, mayonnaise, mustard, cumin and cayenne; set aside. In a large bowl, combine the spinach, cucumber, onions and chicken. Drizzle with yogurt mixture; toss to coat. Microwave pita breads for 15-20 seconds or until warmed. Fill each half with 1/2 cup chicken mixture.

Spinach Pinwheels

Ingredients

(8 ounce) packages refrigerated crescent rolls

(7 ounce) package garlic herb cheese spread

(10 ounce) package frozen chopped spinach, thawed and drained

Directions

Preheat oven to 400 degrees F (200 degrees C).

Split crescent dough in half along center perforation. Flatten one rectangle, sealing perforations. Spread with 1/4 of the cheese spread and sprinkle with spinach. Starting with long side, roll dough up, rolling back and forth several times to seal edges. Cut into 3/4 inch slices (about 15 slices per roll). Arrange the slices one inch apart on ungreased cookie sheet. Continue making the crescent roll ups until all of the ingredients are used.

Bake for 10 to 12 minutes, until lightly browned. Serve immediately or keep warm on a warming tray.

Stuffed Mushrooms with Spinach

Ingredients

2 tablespoons butter
5 slices bacon
1 (10 ounce) package frozen chopped spinach
12 large mushrooms
3 tablespoons butter
2 tablespoons finely chopped onion
2 cloves garlic, peeled and minced
3/8 cup heavy cream
1/4 cup grated Parmesan cheese
salt and pepper to taste
2 tablespoons butter, melted

Directions

Preheat oven to 400 degrees F (200 degrees C). Butter a 9x13 inch baking dish with 2 tablespoons butter.

Place bacon in a large, deep skillet. Cook over medium high heat until evenly brown. Drain, crumble and set aside.

Place frozen spinach in a medium saucepan with 1/4 cup water. Bring water to a boil, then reduce heat to medium and cook spinach covered 10 minutes. Uncover and stir. Remove from heat and drain.

Remove stems from mushrooms. Arrange caps in the baking dish. Finely chop stems.

Melt 3 tablespoons butter in a medium saucepan over medium heat and mix in onion and garlic. Cook 5 minutes, or until tender, then mix in bacon, spinach, chopped mushroom stems and heavy cream. Bring cream to a boil. Remove from heat and mix in Parmesan cheese, salt and pepper.

Stuff mushroom caps generously with the mixture. Drizzle with 2 tablespoons melted butter. Bake in the preheated oven 30 minutes until lightly browned.

Spinach Shrimp Fettuccine

ngredients

pound uncooked fettuccine
(6 ounce) package baby spinach
garlic cloves, minced
tablespoons olive oil
pound uncooked medium
hrimp, peeled and deveined
ripe medium plum tomatoes,
eeded and chopped
/2 teaspoon Italian seasoning
/4 teaspoon salt
/4 cup shredded Parmesan
cheese

Directions

Cook fettuccine according to package directions. Meanwhile, in a large skillet, saute the spinach and garlic in oil for 2 minutes or until spinach begins to wilt. Add the shrimp, tomatoes, Italian seasoning and salt; saute for 2-3 minutes or until shrimp turn pink. Drain fettuccine and add to skillet; toss to coat. Sprinkle with Parmesan cheese.

Spinach, Egg, and Pancetta with Linguine

Ingredients

1 (16 ounce) package uncooked linguine pasta
3 tablespoons olive oil, divided
3 ounces pancetta bacon, diced
1/2 teaspoon crushed red pepper flakes
3 cups loosely packed torn fresh spinach
2 hard-cooked eggs, peeled and chopped
freshly grated Parmesan cheese

Directions

Bring a large pot of salted water to boil. Cook linguine until al dente, about 8 to 10 minutes.

As the water is being brought to boil, heat 1 tablespoon olive oil in a skillet over medium heat. Stir in pancetta, and cook until browned. Remove to paper towels.

Return skillet to heat, and pour in 2 tablespoons olive oil. Stir in crushed red pepper flakes. Then stir in spinach, and cook until softened. Return pancetta to the skillet, and stir in eggs. Cover, and turn off heat.

When the pasta is done, drain, and mix into skillet, reserving some pasta water. If the pasta is too dry, add a small amount of pasta water. Top with freshly grated Parmesan.

Spinach Cheese Strata

Ingredients

/2 cup chopped onion
/4 cup chopped sweet red
epper
/4 cup chopped green pepper
 tablespoons butter or margarine
 (10 ounce) package frozen
hopped spinach, thawed and
ell drained
 cups Wheat Chex® cereal
/2 cup shredded Cheddar
heese
/2 cup shredded Swiss cheese
 eggs
 cups milk
/3 cup crumbled cooked bacon
 teaspoon Dijon mustard
 teaspoon salt
/4 teaspoon white pepper

Directions

In a skillet, saute the onion and peppers in butter until crisp-tender. Remove from the heat. Add spinach and cereal; mix well. Spoon into a greased 11-in. x 7-in. x 2-in. baking dish. Sprinkle with cheese. In a bowl, combine the eggs, milk, bacon, mustard, salt and pepper. Pour over cheese. Bake at 325 degrees F for 45-50 minutes or until knife inserted near the center comes out clean. Let stand for 10 minutes before cutting.

Spinach and Feta Pita Bake

Ingredients

6 (6 inch) whole wheat pita breads
1 (6 ounce) tub sun-dried tomato pesto
2 roma (plum) tomatoes, chopped
1 bunch spinach, rinsed and chopped
4 fresh mushrooms, sliced
1/2 cup crumbled feta cheese
2 tablespoons grated Parmesan cheese
3 tablespoons olive oil
1 pinch ground black pepper to taste

Directions

Preheat the oven to 350 degrees F (175 degrees C).

Spread tomato pesto onto one side of each pita bread, and place them pesto side up on a baking sheet. Top with tomatoes, spinach, mushrooms, feta cheese, and Parmesan cheese. Drizzle with olive oil and season with pepper.

Bake for 12 minutes in the preheated oven or until pita breads are crisp. Cut into quarters and serve.

Quick and Easy Spinach Bread

ngredients

tablespoon olive oil
clove garlic, minced
 (10 ounce) package frozen
hopped spinach, thawed and
rained
 to taste salt and pepper to taste
/4 cup grated Parmesan cheese
arlic powder to taste
 (10 ounce) can refrigerated pizza
rust dough
 cup shredded mozzarella
heese

Directions

Preheat oven to 350 degrees F (175 degrees C). Spray a baking sheet with non-stick cooking spray.

Heat olive oil in a skillet or frying pan over medium heat. Add garlic and saute until soft, about two minutes. Add spinach and cook until liquid has evaporated. Stir in salt, pepper, Parmesan and garlic powder. Remove from heat and let cool.

On a lightly floured surface, roll out pizza crust into a 10x14 inch rectangle. Spread spinach mixture and mozzarella cheese on top of dough. Starting from on end, roll up the crust to make one large loaf. Pinch seam to seal. Place loaf onto prepared baking sheet.

Bake in preheated oven for 20 to 25 minutes, until golden brown.

Spinach and Hazelnut Salad with Strawberry

Ingredients

1/4 cup extra virgin olive oil
1/4 cup aged balsamic vinegar
2 tablespoons sugar-free strawberry preserves
freshly ground black pepper to taste
3 1/2 cups torn fresh spinach
3 1/2 cups romaine lettuce leaves
1/3 cup chopped hazelnuts
1/4 cup golden raisins
1/2 small red onion, thinly sliced 1/2 cup plain mini shredded wheat cereal biscuits
1 ripe avocado, sliced

Directions

In a small bowl, whisk together olive oil, balsamic vinegar, strawberry preserves, and black pepper.

In a large bowl, toss together spinach, lettuce, hazelnuts, raisins, red onion, and shredded wheat biscuits. Drizzle salad dressing over the salad, and toss gently to combine. Serve topped with sliced avocado.

Ingredients

large onion, chopped
garlic clove, minced
teaspoon olive oil
1/2 cups diced cooked chicken
reast meat
(10 ounce) package frozen
hopped spinach, thawed and
queezed dry
/4 cup diced cooked ham
/4 cup grated Parmesan cheese
egg whites
/2 teaspoon dried basil
/8 teaspoon pepper
dash ground nutmeg
2 uncooked manicotti shells
SAUCE:
/4 cup all-purpose flour
cups reduced-sodium chicken
roth
cup fat-free milk
/4 teaspoon salt
/8 teaspoon ground nutmeg
/8 teaspoon pepper
ash cayenne pepper
/4 cup grated Parmesan cheese

Directions

In a small skillet, saute onion and garlic in oil until tender. In a large bowl, combine the onion mixture, chicken, spinach, ham, Parmesan cheese, egg whites, basil, pepper and nutmeg; set aside.

Cook manicotti shells according to package directions. Meanwhile, for sauce, combine flour and broth in a large saucepan until smooth. Stir in the milk, salt, nutmeg, pepper and cayenne. Bring to a boil over medium heat; cook and stir for 2 minutes or until thickened. Spoon 1 cup into chicken mixture. Add Parmesan cheese to remaining sauce.

Spread 1 cup sauce into a 13-in. x 9-in. x 2-in. baking dish coated with nonstick cooking spray. Drain shells; stuff with chicken mixture. Arrange over sauce. Drizzle with remaining sauce. Cover and bake at 375 degrees F for 35-40 minutes or until bubbly and heated through.

Penne Pasta with Spinach and Bacon

Ingredients

1 (12 ounce) package penne pasta
2 tablespoons olive oil, divided
6 slices bacon, chopped
2 tablespoons minced garlic
1 (14.5 ounce) can diced tomatoes
1 bunch fresh spinach, rinsed and torn into bite-size pieces

Directions

Bring a large pot of lightly salted water to a boil. Add the penne pasta, and cook until tender, 8 to 10 minutes.

Meanwhile, heat 1 tablespoon of olive oil in a skillet over medium heat. Place bacon in the skillet, and cook until browned and crisp. Add garlic, and cook for about 1 minute. Stir in the tomatoes, and cook until heated through.

Place the spinach into a colander, and drain the hot pasta over it so it is wilted. Transfer to a large serving bowl, and toss with the remaining olive oil, and the bacon and tomato mixture.

Sausage 'n' Spinach Pockets

Ingredients

/2 pound bulk pork sausage
/3 cup chopped onion
 garlic clove, minced
 cup chopped fresh spinach
/4 cup chopped fresh
nushrooms
/4 cup shredded mozzarella
heese
/2 teaspoon salt
/4 teaspoon pepper
 tablespoons grated Parmesan
heese
 (8 ounce) cans refrigerated
rescent rolls
 egg
 tablespoon water
 tablespoon cornmeal

Directions

In a large skillet, brown sausage, onion and garlic; drain. Remove from the heat; stir in spinach and mushrooms. Add mozzarella cheese, salt, pepper and Parmesan cheese if desired; mix well and set aside. Separate crescent dough into eight rectangles; seal perforations and flatten slightly to 5-in. x 4-1/2-in. rectangles. Place about 1/3 cup sausage mixture on half of each rectangle to within 1/2 in. of edges. Beat egg and water; brush on edges of dough.
Bring unfilled half of dough over filling; press edges with a fork to seal. Brush tops with egg mixture. Sprinkle the cornmeal on a greased baking sheet; place pockets on baking sheet. Bake at 350 degrees F for 15-20 minutes or until golden brown.

Spinach and Apricot-Filled Almond Tarts

Ingredients

Nonstick spray
1 (15 ounce) package ready-made pie crust containing 2 pie crusts (PillsburyB®)
2 tablespoons olive oil
1 clove garlic, minced
10 ounces fresh baby spinach
1/3 cup diced dried apricots
1 tablespoon butter
1/4 teaspoon salt
3 tablespoons slivered California Almonds, roasted*
Special equipment
Dry beans or pie weights
6-inch tart pans with removable bottoms

Directions

Preheat oven to 400 degrees F. Spray 4 tart pans with nonstick spray. Cut pie crusts into fourths, and insert each piece into a tart pan, pressing so it fits and trimming loose ends. Fill with dry beans or pie weights, and bake on a baking sheet 15-20 minutes, or until edges are golden brown. Let cool on rack, and then remove beans or pie weights.

Heat olive oil in a large skillet or wok. Add garlic and simmer on low heat until it turns just a shade darker; turn heat to medium, add spinach and saute, working in 2 batches if pan isnвЪ™t big enough. Gently stir in apricots and butter while spinach is still hot, then sprinkle in almonds.

Fill each tart shell with spinach mixture and serve immediately.

Simple Spinach Lasagna

Ingredients

tablespoon extra virgin olive oil
 (10 ounce) packages frozen
chopped spinach
/2 onion, chopped
/2 teaspoon dried oregano
/2 teaspoon dried basil
 cloves garlic, crushed
 (32 ounce) jar spaghetti sauce
 1/2 cups water
 cups non-fat cottage cheese
 (8 ounce) package part skim
mozzarella cheese, shredded
/4 cup grated Parmesan cheese
/2 cup chopped fresh parsley
 teaspoon salt
/8 teaspoon black pepper
 egg
 ounces lasagna noodles

Directions

Preheat oven to 350 degrees F (175 degrees C).

In a large pot over medium heat saute spinach, onion, oregano, basil and garlic in the olive oil. Pour in spaghetti sauce and water; simmer 20 minutes. In a large bowl mix cottage cheese, mozzarella cheese, Parmesan cheese, parsley, salt, pepper and egg.

Place a small amount of sauce in the bottom of a lasagna pan. Place 4 uncooked noodles on top of sauce and top with layer of sauce. Add 4 more noodles and layer with 1/2 sauce and 1/2 cheese mixture, noodles and repeat until all is layered, finishing with sauce.

Cover with foil and bake in a preheated oven for 55 minutes. Remove foil and bake another 15 minutes. Let sit 10 minutes before serving.

Lightning Source UK Ltd.
Milton Keynes UK
UKHW051020240621
386072UK00002B/193